The 'it' Pit

By Viola & Zaida Stefano

VeeZee Publications

Copyright © VeeZee Publications Pty. Ltd. 2024
First published in Australia in 2024
by VeeZee Publications Pty. Ltd.
veezeepublications.com

The right of Viola Stefano to be identified as the author of this work have been asserted by her in accordance with the **Copyright Amendment (Moral Rights) Act 2000.**

All rights reserved. Apart from any use as permitted by the author & under the **Copyright Act 1968**, no part may be reproduced, copied, scanned, stored in a retrieval system, recorded, or shared, by any means or in any form, without prior written & signed authorization from the publisher.

ISBN: 978-1-923120-10-5

A catalogue record of this book is available from the **National Library of Australia.**

Author: Viola Stefano
Illustrations, cover & internal designs: Zaida Stefano

Illustrations copyright © Zaida Stefano 2024
Design copyright © Zaida Stefano 2024

Disclaimer: The content presented in this book is meant for educational purposes only. The author & publisher claim no accountability to any entity or person for any liability, damage, or loss caused or assumed to be caused directly or indirectly as a consequence of the application, use, or interpretation of the material in this book.

Core words used in this book

I	want	can	stop	look
like	more	he	go	see
here	what	do	the	and
out	where	we	it	up
not	they	when	that	down
she	now	them	is	put
help	off	you	yes	on
turn	who	this	no	why
done	make	a	to	under
come	in	some	which	there
open	get	good	same	home

Come sit down here near the tin fire pit.

It is warm now that it has been lit.

Can you see that moth orbit the flames?

It flits down here, and it flits up there.

I sit still and grit my teeth.

Spin around and look.

Here is the fire pit.

There are more logs. Will they fit into the fire pit?

No! Push that log in a little bit more.

There is the moth. Shoo moth, don't sit there!

Use your wit and do NOT sit.

Little moth, move away from the hot fire pit.

Words with 'it' in this book

it	flits	pit
grit	lit	fit
orbit	bit	wit
	sit	

Words with a short 'i' sound in this book

still	spin	will
is	tin	in

Learning made easy with VeeZee

VeeZee Publications

Wait, there's more!

Visit our website for information about our range of readers & supporting products.

veezeepublications.com

www.ingramcontent.com/pod-product-compliance
Lightning Source LLC
Chambersburg PA
CBHW042107090526
44590CB00004B/123